I THINK AGAIN
OF THOSE
ANCIENT
CHINESE POETS

I THINK AGAIN OF THOSE ANCIENT CHINESE POETS

TOM SEXTON

university of alaska press

fairbanks

University of Alaska Press
P.O. Box 756240
Fairbanks, AK 99775-6240

ISBN 978-1-60223-119-1

Library of Congress Cataloging-in-Publication Data

Sexton, Thomas F.
  I think again of those ancient Chinese poets / Tom Sexton.
    p. cm.
  ISBN 978-1-60223-119-1 (pbk. : alk. paper)
  I. Title.

  PS3569.E88635I13 2011
  811'.54—dc22

                                    2010022908

Cover design by Kristina Kachele

This publication was printed on acid-free paper that meets the mini-
mum requirements for ANSI / NISO Z39.48–
1992 (R2002) (Permanence of Paper for Printed   RECYCLED
Library Materials).   PAPER

For Sharyn, my wife, my muse

ACKNOWLEDGMENTS

Grateful acknowledgements are made to the editors and publishers of the publications in which some of these poems originally appeared: *Albatross*, *The Hudson Review*, *Ice Floe*, *The Northern Review*, and *Wild Apples*.

CONTENTS

Hurricane Station House

We moved in an endless canyon carved in snow
that winter. When the nights were clear, we understood
why the Chinese once called the Milky Way Heaven's
River as it seemed we could hear it flowing overhead,
but what keeps returning to me again and again is how
one night near the station house a handful of willow
ptarmigan, whiter than new snow, rose at our approach,
how our breath caught, how the universe slowed.

Aurora Borealis

When it's cold a foot away from the stove
and the door is rimmed with ice, it's best
to stay inside and read the Chinese poets
and drink another glass or two of wine
unless you sense, and you will, the aurora's
green beginning, then go out and look up
until your head tilts back and your mouth
forms an O like that of a container being filled.

Brown Bear

Yesterday my neighbor saw a brown bear's print
in deep snow that is finally beginning to melt.
Before long we will hear planes that carry hunters,
some dressed all in white, into the high mountains
where bears spend the long winter in their dens.
When they come out, the hunters will be waiting.
Listen, you can hear water flowing beneath snow
and sense buds swelling on cottonwood and birch.

On Our Anniversary

Once again we find ourselves in the woods
where we've walked in weather fair or foul
decade after decade. Is this the life we would
have wished if years ago we'd seen this day:
two people, old to the eye, looking for berries
to pick, hoping the other has a little less luck,
then meeting again, our jeans wet at the knees,
to kneel again beside our overflowing bucket?

Yellow Warblers

At first, the branches of the elderberry
barely move as if touched by a gentle

breeze, then all of a sudden warblers
appear and flow from top to bottom

like the grains of sand in an hourglass.
Would I have seen them this way when

I was young, when time was an endless
loop? They feed for a moment, disappear.

The Wolves of Denali

Let us remember them when we talk of Wilderness
those wolves caught in snares when they wandered
out of Denali's sanctuary, the Garden we allow;
wire from a trapper's snare that didn't hold
is wound tight around the gray's lacerated neck
and the black's face is swollen twice its normal size,
a grotesque mask with one eye missing.
Let us remember them when we talk of Wilderness.

Baneberry

What can be said in praise of the bane-
berry, glowing as red as Mars, as red
as blood, on its stem? Compared
to it the brightest ruby seems dull.

One will stop your heart if swallowed,
but if you have wings and a heart
the size of a drop of rain, it will
nourish you, carry you through the night.

I Think Again of Those Ancient Chinese Poets

Summer with snow still on the mountains
and only a few blossoms on the iris again.

My neighbor wonders why I tend to them year
after year with scant success; to him it's clear

I've failed. I think again of those ancient Chinese poets
who climbed for days to reach an alpine meadow

on the rumor of an iris as dark as the night,
old men calling to each other like cranes in flight.

Winter Night

Tonight the Milky Way's so dense and bright
I imagine that I could touch it if only I

could climb a little higher, reach another
ridge, then I see a wolf's track in the snow,

the track of a gray wolf hunting as it must;
it's as delicate as a blossom newly opened,

and I'm filled with gratitude and wonder:
the Milky Way, a wolf's track in new snow.

Clearing After Snow
Over Mountains and River

After a night of restless sleep, Wang Wei
prepares his brushes and waits for the day

to begin. Not a sound. Not a breath of wind.
The mist rising from his pond will thin

and he will see the heavy snow that fell
on the peaks and silenced the temple's bell,

but for now he sits without a thought
waiting for what will appear and what will not.

Woodcut of a Crane

Its outline cut deep into the wood is firm

and graceful; the deep red of its crown

is that of maple leaves in slant-light

on an autumn afternoon. Notice the wings

cloud-white and spread. Printed on paper

with the texture of grain, it seems to be

standing in the middle of a ripening field.

Listen, you can hear it calling to its mate.

River Otters

At day's end, I was making my way down

from a high ridge that led to the marsh

and the only spot where the ground

was firm enough for me to cross without

sinking into pools of peaty water when

three river otters rose from grass amber

as their pelts and hissed at me before

flowing across the marsh like honey like light.

Thinking of a Friend's Cold Words

After my third glass of wine, after a day
spent brooding over cold words in a letter
from a friend, I think of that Chinese poet
who, when he felt the desire to share a poem,
would build a small wooden boat to carry
it and a gourd of wine down the stream
through rapids to where a recluse lived,
a recluse admired for his long enduring silence.

Snow

Even though it's still Fall, a dense wind-
driven snow has been falling since dawn.
It rises and falls like the wings of a swan,
an image from a fairy tale that begins:
Once upon, but I'm too old for that now,
so I watch it falling beyond my window.
When it slows, I go out to see how deep
it is. It's as light as down, as light as sleep.

Strawberries

I measure friends and strangers by the way
they react when and if I offer one;
delight is what I hope for, a swaying
from side to side, a slight curling of the tongue.

I found them in a long abandoned garden.
Half-wild, they ripen in the shadow of snow.
When cut in half, they show a small white star.
I'll take a few runners with me when I go.

No Moon Tonight

The light is turning blue on the snow
an hour before dusk; a goshawk

is hunting along the edge of the marsh
as it does twilight after twilight.

I light my lamp, listen to its comforting
hiss. The peeling bark of the paper birch

outside my ice-rimmed window will
soon hold the last light. No moon tonight.

Lilac

Even though bees move from strawberry plant

to strawberry plant, the earth has already begun

its slow turn toward winter. I sit by the window

in the generous light of the long day's fading

at the end of my sixty-eighth June.

A fighter plane from the nearby base shakes

the house. War in the year I was born. War now.

Lilac blossoms scent the yard, nod on thin stems.

Grasses in the Marsh

On both sides of the long boardwalk
the marsh grasses are turning russet,

the tallest sway in the slightest breeze
like those followers of Saint Francis who

having given their wealth and noble names
away rose day after day from a bed of twigs

and straw in a peasant's stable or under stars,
heads bowed, swaying like grasses in the marsh.

Yet Another Poem About the Moon

Unable to sleep, I stand in the backyard
listening to the airport where planes from China

are loaded and unloaded throughout the night.
I've come outside to pick berries for breakfast.

Do the cargo handlers ever pause to look
up at the moon so full and bright overhead

that it seems to cover the yard with snow?
The moon Li Po embraced centuries ago.

Glacier

A friend whose poems I criticized after
too much wine loosened my tongue
writes to tell me he has just come back
to town after three days on a glacier, one
he says I cannot see from the window
of the cabin where he knows I often write.
Hard words, but I've been there in a poem.
I was the green-veined ice. I was the night.

Mountain Spinach

Movement in greening alder by the trail
made me think it might be a hungry
bear not long out of its den, but only
an elderly woman with a knife in one hand
appeared. She was picking the new leaves
of the plant I know as watermelon berry.
"Mountain spinach my home Japan," she said.
And then she showed her strong yellow teeth.

Denali

Some fifty years ago, I first saw you rising cold
and forbidding above the other mountains across
Cook Inlet. You were daunting to my eye
that knew only the green rise of mountains
a continent away. Now when I take my morning
walk, I believe that I can see your summit
even when the day is dark and cloudy—
windswept, Communion white, welcoming.

Thinking of a Friend

The newspaper reports deepening cold
to the North, cold enough to make snow
moan beneath your boots when you go
to get water from the stream. Is it frozen

almost to the bottom? Does it rise so
slowly that new ice is beginning to close
the hole you're chopping in slow motion?
Your breath turning white, turning to stone.

August

A week of light rain has turned the woods
to spring again. Only the occasional
devil's club leaf is beginning to turn
yellow, a sheet of papyrus for the heavy
frost that is sure to come; and because it
must, I walk as slowly as I can, pausing
again and again. A shrew darts across
the trail into the alder's soft green fist.

To Wang Wei

Last night, I walked beside the inlet
to wait for the moon that was still behind

the mountains to appear. It was very cold
so I was alone with my thoughts of you

and your immortal poems. When it rose,
the moon was round and paler than my

breath. We are small waves breaking
on the shore and just as soon forgotten.

An Empty Bowl

For several days now I've been watching
a cloud of sulfurous smoke from coal-
burning plants in far away Hunan Province
darken over the glacial mountains that curve
toward Asia like the tail of a mythical dragon.
Last night, I sat by the window reading Li Po
until the moon's broken yolk disappeared.
My hair's white. My heart's an empty bowl.

Arctic Char

Under a cut bank not far from where Pass Creek
flows under a railroad trestle, char will take a wet
fly if you cast upstream so the current carries it
to them, but it's better to just kneel and watch
for the small orange spots on their turning sides.
Glacier-carved falls end their world to the west.
A chain of beaver ponds begins it to the east.
Why spend our lives longing for another world?

Crossing a Marsh by Train

Grown heavy with sweet fat
from a season of eating salmon

and berries, a brown bear
ambling across the wide marsh

pauses to watch our approach,
its silvery hump

like a thin crescent of moon.
And then we are gone.

Watching Winter Light
from Chulitna Butte

Below me, light ebbs from the wide marsh

toward stand after stand of paper birch,

salt-white for a moment before they darken.

I watch as the glacial mountains that rise

beyond the Chulitna River to the west

begin to glow. It's as if the light opened

a door that only it can enter. When I start

down, the Fairbanks train is curving into itself.

Morning Landscape, Early Spring

Thin green leaves are opening
in the woods above the inlet's

silted water, brown as the coat
of the bear, snout down digging

for something to eat, I saw a few
days after the last snow melted.

The creaking-hinge of migrating
cranes will fill the air before long.

Coming Down from
the Mountains into Mist

Following a path leading down from a ridge

people climb to look out over the still quiet city

to the snow covered mountains, I can see mist

beginning to form where rivulets come together

to become a stream and then a small pond

as round and white as the moon when full.

When I reach the stream, the mist is so dense

it could be a Chinese scroll unrolling inch by inch.

No Time for Metaphor

He smiled and said the ring around the moon
was its own light reflecting
from ice crystals in the atmosphere
or a smoke ring blown by you know who.

She frowned and said it was the shawl
the woman in the moon
wore only on the coldest of nights
or it was not worth mentioning at all.

Ephemeral

Dragonflies catching the morning light,
making it glow copper and bluish-green,
making it visible the way stained glass
made it visible to a child sitting in a pew
many years ago. I watch them move as one
over a grassy swale that was a vernal pool
not long ago. If I come this way tomorrow
they will be gone. Even if I come at dawn.

Ermine

It is no longer weasel:
not to be trusted, blood thirsty,
sneak, double crosser,
herald of death, deceiver.

Wearing its winter pelt of white,
it's the season's cursive line
flowing over pliant snow;
black-tipped tail as exclamation point.

Leaving Again

On the high ridges above stands of birch
where from time to time you can see a seam
of coal or one of copper, the tundra will be deep
red by now. Leaving is no longer a burr
under my tongue. Before we reach the small
lake where migrating swans rest for the night,
I'll turn to ask you once again if you recall
how when they rose at dawn our hearts took flight?

Washington County, Maine

Apple trees heavy with the season's fruit,
piebald, yellow, planet-red, even black,
stand abandoned in fields, the unintended
gift of those who long ago moved on,
a gift to waxwings and even to the tone-
deaf crows in their undertaker's suits,
to the man driving slowly, window down,
to the worms in their snow-white orbit.

By Passamaquoddy Bay

Thin light over Campobello Island
to the east when I rise to walk
the long abandoned railroad bed.
Not a trace is left of the rails.
I have several letters to answer
and yesterday's paper to read,
but the wild apples are waiting
cold on the tongue, polished by mist.

Witch Hazel

Deep in a wood, I watch a witch hazel
swaying from side to side as if it were
a dowser moving a rod over the ground,
but no one fallen under its spell will
appear to cut a forked branch, or peel
it slowly to reveal the bright wood,
no one will test its weight and balance,
be dark water flowing through stone.

Starlings

In allegorical times, they would be the angry
crowd swirling down a narrow street at dusk
hissing like a river surging over its banks,
the beaked figures in a medieval painting
there to remind us Man is fallen, if not damned;
but, now they are black birds roosting in a leaf-
less New England oak, nursing the memory
of a cage in a ship's dark hold, the alien light.

Late Afternoon

In a clearing on a slope beside the bay
where an apple tree with wind forged
branches has stood decade after decade,
the winter grass glowed as if it were copper

polished by the willing light, then branch
by branch the tree began to glow. As I
watched, a hawk, also copper colored,
rose with a rabbit in its glowing talons.

Robert Frost in Winter

This will always be his, this stand of white
birch, every branch coated with ice
from a storm that began in the night as snow.
He is alone. No one else is on the road.
No climbing or swinging now. Only the crack
of branches beginning to fall to the ground
so that before long the ice is a burial mound
fit for his grief. There is no turning back.

Larch

They stand in the middle of the marsh
without a needle on a single branch,
indifferent to the man walking toward them
who is looking for holly to cut for his wife.
They dream of a strong arm, a pitch-black axe,
of Vikings roaring between their supple ribs,
who carved dragons' heads from their hearts
and cleaved the ocean's white-tongued waves.

Blackberries

When I saw the grass touched by frost
I knew it was time to pick the blackberries
hidden from sight at the end of the marsh.
A light frost seems to make them sweeter
and heavy frost ends their season overnight.
The first blackberry that I put in my mouth
was as black as the noisy crows overhead,
as sweet as the first halting kiss of a lover.

Sedge Wren

A tiny bird seldom seen in this place
appears for a moment in tall grass
before it disappears from sight—
a handful of air, the rustle of leaves.
If I were a spirit or even a ghost,
this is how I would appear to the world:
wearing a coat of modest feathers,
filling the air with melodious sound.

Winterberry Holly

Look for it where the ground is wet,

marsh and bog are best. It's leafless

by November so you can easily cut

the branches heavy with red berries.

One morning when I was on my knees

looking at small tracks beneath the one

I was going to cut, perhaps had begun

to cut, I saw a galaxy spun from seed.

Tu Fu

I think of you wandering those snow-choked
mountains between warring armies long ago

with only hunger in your belly. A man picking
snails from a rocky spit for a rich man's table

was lost to the quickly rising tide tonight
not far from where I write. The poor are still

as numerous as the stars in the sky above
and endless war is still our one-eyed destiny.

House Sparrows

No one will ever call Audubon or a friend
to report a sighting of these small chestnut-
hued birds rushing in and out of a hole
left when worn bricks fell from the side of
a building itself about to fall; yet they
have their calling, like the now rare working
man in his canvas jacket leaving the house
before dawn, the first hint of song on the street.

Decoy of a Snow Goose

Carved from yellow cedar, it seems lighter
than air, lighter than the swirling flakes
that gives it its name. Tallow candle white.
The carver's knife has feathered the grain.

When I hold it in my hand, I see snow geese
against the gathering clouds of an autumn
storm over Pounce Coupe Prairie, a skein
coming down in a swirl. Thunder like a drum.

Pasque Flower

As we drove north, lake after lake,
absent spring's migrating swans

and dark water, seemed locked
forever in an icy stare, as if this

stasis were our destination, then
we saw the pasque flower with its

belled promise by the side of the road
and heard the sound of water flowing.

Traveler's Moon

Home again. I'm reading Po Chu-i's poem
about the moon that was a mere crescent

when the traveler in his poem set out
centuries ago to begin his long journey.

Three times he watched it round to full.
When I get up from my chair to join my

wife in bed, I can see his moon over
the mountains across the inlet, over Denali.

Alder Thicket

Beside the busy road, alders so dense
they seem to be woven together, a branch

quivers and then an unseen warbler's
song, each leaf a green boat waiting

for its journey to begin, kinglet's drinking
cup, spirit's lantern, wind's hammock—

pale smoke, wet wood burning, roof
of a homeless camp, rope of sorrow.

Equinox

If I were a young black bear when snow
first appears on the mountains the way

it did when I woke, I'd climb the nearest
chokecherry tree and gorge on its ripe

fruit until my stomach was full and taut
like a drum. Leaving tree after tree bent

to the ground in my wake, I'd wobble away
to sleep in a cave with twigs in my hair.

Su Tung P'o

I take down a favorite book of poetry from
my shelf and turning to a well-thumbed page
join him once again on the winding path
to a mountain lake that becomes the moon
then the lake again when we rise from sleep.
Over our balding heads, cloud-minnows swim,
and all around us the wilderness spreads out—
peak after jagged peak touching the stars.

Bohemian Waxwings

I've seen them sitting in leafless trees
at dusk like monks at their prayers

or at dawn like gossips in their finest dress
bringing word of berries that stain the tongue.

The sound of their wings when they rise
as one from a tree reminds me of the sea

but it's the stillness when they're gone
that makes me long each year for their return.

Liqueur

Before long, we will be too old to crawl

under fallen trees where currants grow

too old to make our way through spiny

devil's club that can slice skin like a razor

blade to pick ripe berries like the ones

we use to make this ruby-red liqueur

so let us drink one glass too many tonight.

Notice how it loves the moon, how sad it is.

A Painting of the Poet Meng Hao Jan

Wearing a bright red cloak that ends just
above his worn boots, he sits on the back
of a small donkey. They face tall mountains
with endless peaks where they will wander
both day and night through drifts of snow
with the donkey's bell the only familiar sound
until they come to the year's first flowering plum
its white blossoms opening on a leafless branch.

For Frances Gramse, Age 3, on the Winter Solstice

New snow has turned the world white
as far as the eye can see. It will cover
your father's shoulders when he comes
in with his arms full of wood to keep
you warm tonight; sleep well, the cold
and the dark will fade and the lake
will open its eye. Grebes will arrive.
Always align your heart with the light.

Winter Landscape: Fish Creek

No kingfisher falls like a blue-gray
arrow. Ice covers the tidal creek,

new ice that will split with a hiss
when the tide begins to come in.

A novice at seventy, I still lean
over the rail to watch its rise

and fall. Harnessed to the moon,
it doesn't have a worry in the world.

To Wang Wei After Reading
a New Translation of His Poems

How bright the world an hour before dawn.

Yesterday's bare ground is covered with snow

that fell while I slept and is falling still.

Pearl-white clouds glow from deep within.

They fill the room with their luminous light.

I put the kettle on and sit by the window.

I'm a glow worm who from time to time

thought he was the moon until I read your poems.